Cleo
For Salicylate Intolerance

Recipes
developed and illustrated by
Linda Donald

One of the best days of my life was also one of the worst. It was the day I finally discovered why I had been feeling unwell, but also that I could not eat many of my favourite foods if I wanted to feel better.

What had been making me ill was a salicylate intolerance which played havoc with my well being.

I love yummy things to eat and come from a family where cooking is a passion. I don't have formal qualifications, but have enjoyed a lifetime of preparing and sharing all sorts of delicious recipes.

I was shattered. How could I travel, go out to restaurants or cook for family and friends? Would I ever eat properly again?

I decided I would just have to find ways to make the food I loved with ingredients I could eat.

This cookbook is the result of trial and error, adapting many of the dishes we had always loved to eat, by replacing or reducing their salicylate content. As well as giving you a selection of easy to follow recipes, I have included a list of substitutes to try as replacements for salicylate high or very high ingredients.

If you find you have a salicylate intolerance, I hope this collection of recipes will help you enjoy cooking and eating again.

By cooking from scratch, you will also avoid preservatives and additives, which may also upset you.

The dietician explained how there is not a lot of difference between low and moderate salicylate foods, but a big jump up to high and more so to very high.

In "Clever Cooking", I have used only foods that are moderate or less. It's amazing what you can create with just a few cleverly combined ingredients.

Please let me know how you get on. I would love to hear what works for you, along with any suggestions you may have.

I hope it gives you back one of life's greatest pleasures.

Happy cooking!

Best wishes,

Linda
ldonald@imagesandwords.co.nz
www.salicylate.org

P.S. Sally, the little cartoon figure who appears throughout, shows how the right recipes will take you from feeling sick and miserable to the joy of feeling a zest for life again.

CONTENTS

Breakfast 5

Starters and Lunch 15

Soups 29

Main Course 33
    Fish
    Meat
    Poultry

Rice, Pasta, Eggs 51

Vegetables and Salads 61

Baking 75

Desserts 89

Jams and Chutneys 97

Dressings, Sauces, Spreads, Stock 101

Substitutes and Tips 107

General 109

Index 110

BREAKFAST OPTIONS

As well as the recipes in the breakfast section, any of the following make excellent breakfast choices: -

Cereals - Special K, All Bran, Bran Flakes, Puffed Wheat or Rice Bubbles with hot or cold milk, sugar or maple syrup.

Crumpets with melted butter or toasted and popped under the grill with some grated cheese.

Eggs, poached, scrambled, baked (see page 6) or fried on suitable toast, or in an omelette.

Porridge made from rolled oats, sprinkled with sugar and milk.

Rye or wholemeal toast, with cream cheese and/or pear jam and/or maple cashew butter.

BREAKFAST

BAKED EGGS IN INDIVIDUAL DISHES
(Oeufs en cocotte)

4 eggs
8 tablespoons cream
2 tablespoons softened butter
Salt to taste

Pre-heat oven to 350F/180C.

Butter 4 small ramekins and break an egg into each dish.

Season with salt and spoon 2 tablespoons of cream over each egg.

Bake in oven 6-8 minutes till firm.

For a delicious light lunch, put a tablespoon of finely grated cheese and/or shredded ham or chicken on base of dish before putting in the egg.

BIRCHER MEUSLI

2 cups rolled oats
1 x 410gm/13ozs tin pears in syrup
½ cup water
½ cup natural yoghurt

Mix together rolled oats, syrup from pears (1 cup), water and finely chopped tinned pears.

Cover and put in fridge over night.

Take out, add yoghurt and mix well.

For delicious options, add a a handful of chopped raw cashews and/or a drizzle of maple syrup and/or sliced banana.

BREAKFAST FRUIT, YOGHURT AND MAPLE SYRUP

Combine fresh pawpaw, banana, pear and/or moderate - mango, gala/pacific rose/golden or red delicious apple, tamarillo (tree tomato) and persimmon.

Served topped with plain thick yoghurt, drizzled with maple syrup.

Sprinkling with a handful of Special K, All Bran, Bran Flakes, Puffed Wheat or Rice Bubbles makes a perfect crunchy addition.

CROQUE MONSIEUR
Serves 4

French dish of toasted bread with cheese, ham or bacon and a creamy sauce.

8 slices rye, wholemeal, white or French bread
4 slices ham or 4 cooked rashers of nitrite free, free range bacon

CREAMY SAUCE

2 cups milk
2 tablespoons butter or rice bran spread
2 tablespoons flour (all purpose or rice flour for a light creamy sauce)
1 cup grated tasty cheese (a white goat or ewe's cheese is excellent)
Pinch of salt

Melt butter or rice bran spread in medium saucepan. Whisk in flour and salt till bubbling and cook, whisking all the time for about 5 minutes. Add milk and whisk till smooth and thick about 5 minutes. Add ¾ of cheese and salt and stir over low heat to melt.

Pre heat oven grill. Make sauce. Toast slices of bread. Place a slice of ham or bacon on 4 slices of bread. Cover each one with creamy sauce, using half the sauce. Place another piece of bread on top and cover each using rest of sauce. Sprinkle each with a share of the remaining ¼ cup of cheese and place under grill till bubbling and golden.

FRENCH TOAST

6 slices thick white bread
½ cup milk
3 eggs
2 tablespoons butter for cooking

Beat milk and eggs together in a shallow dish. Dip each slice of bread into egg/milk mixture until fully coated.

Pan fry 2 slices at a time in a third of the butter melted in a heated frying pan. Brown slices on both sides, cooking till set.

For a sweet version, add ½ cup of sugar and 1 teaspoon of vanilla essence to basic mixture, beating well till sugar is dissolved.

HASH BROWNS

4 large waxy roasting/all purpose potatoes peeled
½ cup rice bran or canola oil
1 dessertspoon finely chopped parsley
Salt to taste

Boil potatoes 8 - 10 minutes, so they are still firm. Remove from heat, drain and leave till cool.

Grate coarsely into a bowl, stir in parsley and season with salt. You will find the potatoes are sticky to handle.

Heat about 2 tablespoons oil at a time in a frying pan and drop rounded tablespoons of potato mixture into pan.

Flatten each hash brown with a fork or spatula and cook for a few minutes on each side on medium heat till golden.

Makes about 20 and I use two frying pans to save time.

Serve by themselves or with bacon or smoked salmon.

PANCAKES

1 cup flour
1 cup milk
1 egg
About 1 tablespoon butter
Pinch of salt

Beat all ingredients together till smooth. Add a little more milk if too thick.

Melt dob of butter in frying pan.

Spoon about ¼ cup of mixture for each pancake into pan and cook 2 to 3 minutes until lightly brown underneath.

Turn over and cook till mixture is set and this side is lightly brown too.

Serve lightly buttered or with bananas and maple syrup and/or yoghurt.

Makes about 8 pancakes.

WAFFLES

Your waffle maker, plus the following ingredients: -

1 cup flour
1 heaped teaspoon baking powder
Pinch salt
1 ½ tablespoons sugar
2 eggs, separated
¾ cup milk
75gms/2 ½ ozs melted rice bran spread or butter

In a large bowl, sift in flour, baking powder and salt.
Add sugar and stir.

Make a well in centre of dry ingredients and add lightly beaten egg yolks, milk and melted bran spread or butter.

Beat till smooth.

Fold in stiffly beaten egg whites.

Use 3 tablespoons of batter for each waffle - enough for 5 delicious light waffles.

To serve, spoon over thick plain yoghurt and maple syrup or try finely sliced banana, cubed pawpaw or slices of peeled pear with a dash of maple syrup.

STARTERS
& LUNCH

CREPES
Thin French pancake for savoury or sweet fillings

1 egg
150 mls/5 fluid ozs water
150 mls/5 fluid ozs milk
6 rounded tablespoons plain flour
Savoury - pinch of salt, or
Sweet - teaspoon pure vanilla essence

Sift flour and put with rest of ingredients in a bowl. Beat till completely smooth with electric beater.

This recipe does not need to stand before making crepes, but if you do, add another tablespoon of water before using.

To make crepes, melt a tiny amount of butter (about ⅓ teaspoon) in a crepe pan or medium frying pan, swirl around to coat bottom of pan.

Add 2 to 3 tablespoons of batter and move pan till bottom is evenly coated. Cook a minute or two till edges of crepe come away from side of pan and bottom is lightly brown.

Flip over with a metal spatula and cook a minute on the other side. Remove from pan and make next crepe. Stack crepes on top of each other on a plate.

Makes about 8 crepes, depending on size of pan.

CREPE FILLINGS

Fillings can be made in advance and frozen.
Sauce for six to eight crepes.

SAUCE BASE

2 tablespoons butter
1 spring onion, finely chopped
1 rounded tablespoon flour
½ cup milk or cream
Pinch of salt
¾ cup grated tasty cheese

Melt butter in a medium sized pot. Add a finely chopped spring onion and cook a minute or two till soft. Add flour. Cook for 2 to 3 minutes, whisking to mix.

Gradually add milk or cream. Whisk till thick and smooth. Season with salt. Add half of tasty cheese and stir over low heat till melted.

FOR CHICKEN FILLING

1 cup cooked chicken, cut in small pieces
1 dessertspoon parsley finely chopped
Optional - 3 rashers of cooked bacon,
    cut in small pieces

Add chicken and parsley, plus bacon if being used, to sauce and mix well.

A splash of vodka or whisky gives a lovely flavour and will thin sauce if it is too thick.

CREPE FILLINGS
(CONTINUED)

FOR VEGETARIAN FILLING

½ teaspoon miso paste

1 leek, finely chopped

½ cup fresh green peas, steamed till just cooked, or ½ cup of frozen peas, thawed

2 medium old season potatoes, peeled, cooked and chopped in small pieces

Same sauce base, but omit spring onion and add miso paste for taste. Pan fry leek till soft and add to prepared sauce with green peas and potatoes. Add a touch of water if sauce too thick.

Brussels sprouts can be used instead of peas or as an extra ingredient. Other options, either as combinations or by themselves, are cooked asparagus, pumpkin and/or carrot (all moderate).

Fill centre of crepes with chosen filling and roll up. Put in oven proof dish in single layer.

Sprinkle each with a share of remaining grated cheese and pop in oven under grill a few minutes till cheese is melted and golden.

FILLINGS FOR CROISSANTS, PITA POCKETS, SANDWICHES, ROLLS, WRAPS

SPREAD ANY OF THE ABOVE WITH -

Cream cheese, pear sauce (see page 102), parsley pesto (see page 22) or roast garlic hummus (see page 22)

ADD

Cooked chicken, turkey, ham, bacon, lamb or beef; tuna, salmon, or grated cheese

PLUS ONE OR A COMBINATION OF

Finely sliced cabbage (Savoy is particularly sweet) or red cabbage, chopped celery, diced spring onions, mung bean sprouts, shredded iceberg lettuce, sliced or fork mashed boiled egg or grated beetroot and/or carrot (carrot and beetroot are moderate)

Combine filling with a little suitable salad dressing or mayonnaise.

MINI QUICHE IN BREAD CASES

12 slices bread (white, wholemeal, bran or grain without nuts or seeds)
Rice bran spread to cover bread slices
3 standard size eggs
125gms/4ozs feta, crumbled
60gms/2ozs tasty goat's cheese
100mls/3 fluid ozs cream
Level dessertspoon finely chopped parsley.

12 standard size muffin tray

Preheat oven to 180C/350F.

Butter slices of bread with rice bran spread. Cut round shape from each slice using 3cm/2inch cutter. Push a round into each muffin tray compartment buttered side down till it fits snugly.

Bake 10 minutes in preheated oven till crisp. Take out of oven and leave in muffin tray.

Combine, beaten eggs with crumbled feta, grated cheese, cream and parsley. Fill each case with egg mixture. Return to oven and bake about 20 minutes till set and golden.

Serve as a snack or with pear sauce (see page 102) or tamarillo chutney (moderate) (see page 100) and fresh salad for a yummy light lunch.

NACHOS WITH MINCE, SOUR CREAM AND CHEESE

Savoury mince (see page 38)
Home made pita crisps (see page 24), or
Bagel crisps, or
Corn chips or Tacos (both moderate)

½ cup lite sour cream
1 cup grated tasty cheese
1 tablespoon finely chopped chives

Arrange crisps of your choice on serving platter and top with hot mince mixture, then grated cheese, sour cream and sprinkling of chopped chives.

You can also serve by surrounding a serving of mince with crisps of your choice and topping mince with cheese, sour cream and chives.

This is great served as one dish to share or as individual portions.

PARSLEY PESTO

1 cup lightly packed parsley leaves
1 teaspoon citric acid
1 cup raw cashew nuts
1 teaspoon salt
½ cup rice bran oil
2 tablespoons finely grated parmesan cheese (optional)

Put parsley and citric acid in food processor and process. Add nuts and salt, process until well blended. With motor running, drizzle rice bran oil to form pesto paste.

Great as a dip for pita crisps (see page 24).

ROAST GARLIC HUMMUS

2 medium heads garlic
2 x 398ml/13oz approx tins chick peas
1 rounded teaspoon citric acid
¾ teaspoon salt
1 dessertspoon finely chopped parsley (optional)
½ cup or so rice bran oil (enough to give hummus the consistency you want)

Slice tip of garlic head and drizzle with bran oil. Roast 30 minutes in medium oven (180C/350F) till soft. Let cool. Squeeze soft flesh out of garlic pieces.

Drain and rinse chick peas. Blend garlic and chick peas in food processor with citric acid and salt till not quite smooth.

Add rice bran oil to suit and blend to consistency you want. Stir in parsley.

Serve with suitable bagel crisps.

Both of these are delicious with your own home baked pita crisps (see page 24)

PITA CRISPS

8 mini oat bran or plain mini pita bread (unleavened flat breads) with no preservatives or additives
Bran oil for spraying
2-3 cloves fresh garlic, crushed - optional
Rock salt - optional

Carefully split each pita bread into two rounds. Cut each round into four triangles. Spray uneven side with rice bran oil. Put onto baking tray, smooth side down.

Sprinkle with a little crushed rock salt and/or garlic before baking.

Bake in pre-heated oven 15 to 20 minutes at 150C/300F till golden.

Serve as they are or with roast garlic hummus as a dip.

PIZZA WITH HOMEMADE BASE

Makes one large pizza or 2 regular

1 tablespoon dry yeast
2 teaspoons sugar
2 ½ cups flour
1 tablespoon finely chopped parsley
300mls/10 fluid ozs luke warm water
3 tablespoons rice bran oil

BASE

Blend yeast and sugar in a small bowl. Add a little of the warm water and mix well. Add rest of water and set aside a few minutes till frothy.

Combine flour and parsley in a large bowl. Make a well in centre and pour in yeast liquid plus 2 tablespoons of oil.

Mix to form a firm dough and set aside somewhere warm until about double in size. (Takes an hour or so in hot water cupboard with tea towel over top of bowl).

Punch down, roll into one or two rounds and push into oiled pizza baking try. Brush top with 1 tablespoon oil.

TOPPINGS

1 cup lightly packed parsley leaves
3 tablespoons grated parmesan cheese
⅓ cup rice bran oil

Process all together to form a rough paste. Spread over pizza base.

Add any of the following then spray with canola or rice bran oil before putting in oven.

- Cubes of peeled old season potato and strips of bacon, topped with grated gruyere cheese.
- Slices of peeled and finely sliced old season potato sprinkled with finely chopped garlic and spring onions.
- A leek finely diced and lightly cooked in a little oil till soft, topped with ham and small cubes of feta cheese.
- Pieces of cooked chicken, peas and spring onions, topped with tasty grated cheese.
- Scatter with prawns and a little pawpaw. Top with some finely grated medium cheese.
- Moderate additions or combinations, are blanched snow peas, asparagus and cubes of cooked pumpkin or sweet potato.

Preheat oven to 200C/390F.

Cook for about 40 minutes till base cooked and topping golden.

Sprinkle cooked pizza with finely chopped chives before serving.

QUICHE WITH HOMEMADE BASE

Enough for one very large or one medium and one small base

2 cups flour
3 rounded teaspoons baking powder
185gms/6ozs butter
1 egg yolk
¼ to ½ cup cold milk
Pinch of salt

Pre-heat oven to 190C/375F. Sift flour into a bowl and rub in butter until like fine breadcrumbs. Add salt and stir. Make a hollow in centre and drop in lightly beaten egg yolk and mix. Add milk little by little until you make a ball that sticks together.

Remove from bowl and roll out pastry on floured surface to ¼ inch thick / ½ cm. Place in pie dish or dishes and trim to fit. Put in fridge for half an hour. Fill with prepared filling and bake 45 minutes or until set.

FILLING BASE

Mix together 1 ½ cups of cream, 4 lightly beaten eggs, pinch of salt, ½ cup grated cheese

FILLING OPTIONS

- Leek - 2 finely chopped leeks softened in 1 tablespoon butter
- Quiche Lorraine (bacon and cheese) - 4 rashers of bacon diced and pan fried in tablespoon rice bran oil or ½ cup finely diced ham
- Vegetable - cup of any or combination of diced cooked beans/green peas/Brussels sprouts/chives/old season potato or moderate - pumpkin/kumera or sweet potato/parsnip/carrot/asparagus

TOASTED TARTINE

½ French stick or baguette
2 tablespoons pear sauce (see page 102) or
   tamarillo chutney (moderate) (see page 100)
1 cup grated cheese (tasty/gouda/gruyere)
12 small cubes feta cheese
2 thick slices ham, cubed
1 egg

Preheat oven to 180C/350F.

Cut bread stick through middle, then each half into three pieces. Spread each with pear sauce or tamarillo chutney.

Lightly beat egg and combine with cup of grated cheese and cubed ham. Top each piece of bread with cheese/ham mixture. Dot with cubes of feta.

Bake 5 to 10 minutes.

Reduce oven to 120C/250F and cook further 10 minutes till cheese mixture is set and golden.

You can use grill for a minute or two at end.

Great way to use up any remaining French stick or baguette.

SOUPS

CHICKEN SOUP
Pot chicken stock (see page 105)

½ cup barley
½ leek, finely diced
2 cloves garlic, crushed
1 tablespoon canola oil

1 stick celery, finely chopped
2 sprigs parsley, finely chopped
½ carrot (moderate/optional)
½ parsnip (moderate/optional)
1 cup finely chopped cooked chicken
1 rounded teaspoon miso paste

To strained chicken stock and chopped chicken meat used to make stock, add barley, bring to the boil and simmer 45 minutes.

Heat little canola oil in small saucepan. Add crushed garlic and leek and toss till golden. Add to stock and barley.

Finely dice celery, parsley, carrot and parsnip and add to stock together with cup of cubed chicken and miso paste. Cook further 15 minutes.

Serve with crusty warm bread.

GREEN PEA & LETTUCE SOUP

2 cups frozen baby peas
3 spring onions, finely sliced
2 cloves garlic, peeled and crushed
60gms/2ozs rice bran spread or butter
Pinch sea salt
2 cups hot water mixed with 1 tablespoon miso paste
1 iceberg lettuce - hard centre removed and cut into 10 or so pieces
¼ cup cream, sour cream or finely grated parmesan cheese to decorate
1 tablespoon finely chopped chives.

Add peas to hot water, miso and salt in a medium saucepan and boil for 5 minutes. While peas are cooking, melt butter or rice bran spread in large pot and lightly panfry spring onions and garlic for 2 to 3 minutes. Continuing to stir, add lettuce pieces and cook for another 2 to 3 minutes till leaves are wilted.

Add pea mixture to lettuce mixture and cook gently for another 2 to 3 minutes. Cool slightly, then process in food processor to a coarse puree.

Serve hot, topped with a swirl of cream, spoon of sour cream or little finely grated parmesan cheese. Finish with a fine sprinkling of chopped chives.

This soup has a delicious nutty flavour and can also be served in little cups as an appetite teaser, or for lunch with hot home-made damper (see page 86)

Serves 4

LEEK & POTATO SOUP
VICHYSSOISE

2 medium leeks, finely sliced (all the white and a little of the green)
2 spring onions, finely chopped
2 tablespoons butter
2 large old season white potatoes, peeled and cut in small pieces
1 tablespoon miso
6 cups hot water
1 tablespoon chopped parsley
teaspoon sea salt
½ cup cream
Parsley to garnish

Melt butter and cook leeks and spring onions on medium heat till tender. Add potatoes and parsley, hot water and miso. Simmer for 20 minutes till potatoes are tender. Take off heat and cool a little.

Put in food processor and process till smooth and creamy. Add cream and salt to taste.

To serve swirl a tablespoon of whipped or sour cream on top of each serving and sprinkle with a little extra finely chopped parsley.

In summer, a delicious alternative is to serve this soup cold.

Serves 4 to 6

MAIN COURSE

FISH | MEAT | POULTRY

BEEF CASSEROLE

1kg/2lb blade, chuck, topside or rump steak
4 cloves garlic, finely chopped
1 tablespoon parsley, finely chopped
½ carrot, peeled and diced (moderate)
1 stick celery, diced finely
1 small leek, finely chopped
2 slices bacon, finely chopped
3 tablespoons rice bran oil
1 tablespoon butter
2 tablespoon miso
2 cups hot water
1 tablespoon pear sauce (see page 102) or
    tamarillo chutney (moderate) (see page 100)

2 large old season potatoes cut in serving
    size pieces
1 cup frozen peas
1 carrot cut in serving size pieces (moderate)
2 parsnips cut in serving size pieces (moderate)
1 teaspoon or more of cornflour with water
    to mix
Extra finely chopped chives for decoration

Pre-heat oven to 180C/350F.

Toss cubed beef in flour. Heat 2 tablespoons oil in stove-to-oven pot on stove top and in 2 batches panfry beef until golden, approximately 5 minutes.

Remove from pan. Add 1 tablespoon oil and butter and brown bacon and garlic. Add leek, parsley, finely diced carrot and celery and cook about 5 minutes stirring all the time to infuse flavours. Add miso paste and pear sauce or tamarillo chutney with hot water and stir well. Return beef and juices to pot. Make sure liquid covers contents, so add more water if necessary.

Cover pot and cook in oven for 30 minutes. Stir and add potatoes, carrot, parsnip and peas. Cover and return to oven for 1 to 1 ½ hours with the occasional stir to ensure casserole does not stick to bottom of pot. Thicken sauce with cornflour and water if required. A splash of whisky can be added at the end to give a special flavour.

Serve sprinkled with finely chopped chives.

Serves 6

Accompany with steamed Brussels sprouts, fresh green beans or asparagus. Some or all of the moderate ingredients can be omitted.

LAMB SHANKS

4 lamb shanks
4 tablespoons flour
3 tablespoons canola oil
1 leek, finely chopped (just white part)
2 cloves garlic, finely chopped
1 tablespoon chopped parsley
1 celery stalk, finely chopped
½ carrot, finely chopped (moderate)
1 cup cooked brown lentils

1 tablespoon miso
2 cups hot water
Salt

Preheat oven to 200C/400F.

Roll shanks in flour. Heat oil in stove-top to oven pot and brown lamb shanks all over (about 10 minutes). Add leeks, garlic, parsley, celery and carrot and cook till leek has softened. Add hot water with miso and stir. Cover and cook in oven for one hour.

Add lentils and cook another 30 minutes, until meat is nearly falling off the bone.

Season with salt to taste and serve with mashed potatoes, beans, peas or Brussels sprouts or a green salad.

Serves 4

MEAT OR CHICKEN BALLS

500gms/1lb lean beef, lamb, pork or chicken mince
1 dessertspoon miso paste
1 stick celery, very finely diced
3 cloves fresh garlic, peeled and fine diced
2 pieces crustless rye bread soaked 5 minutes in
   water, then squeezed dry and crumbled

Preheat oven to 180C/350F.

Combine all ingredients well. Form meat mixture into walnut sized balls. Place on greased baking tray and bake for 20 to 25 minutes till golden, turning after 15 minutes.

Serve with pear sauce (see page 102) or tamarillo chutney (moderate) (see page 100) and potato souffle (see page 91)

Make larger patties and serve as hamburgers with coleslaw (see page 63).

SAVOURY MINCE

For pita pockets, flat bread wraps, a toasted sandwich, on toast or in bread baskets.

500gms/1lb lean mince (beef, or chicken or lamb or combination of lamb and beef)
1 carrot, peeled and finely diced (moderate)
3 spring onions, finely chopped
2 stalks celery, finely chopped
3 cloves fresh garlic, peeled and finely chopped
2 tablespoons finely chopped parsley
1 tablespoon miso
1 tablespoon brufax (yeast flakes) - optional
½ to ⅔ cup of water
Little rice bran oil for cooking

Heat oil in large saucepan. Add garlic, ¼ of parsley, celery, carrot and spring onion and cook till garlic is slightly golden. Add mince and break up with wooden spoon. Continue stirring till meat is cooked. Add rest of carrot, spring onion, celery and garlic with miso and water.

Cook all together, stirring from time to time, till liquid has nearly all gone, about 20 minutes.

Add brufax (if you like) and stir into meat mixture.

FILLING FOR PITA POCKETS OR SUITABLE FLAT BREAD

Prepared savoury mince
6 pita pockets or suitable flat breads
1 cup shredded lettuce or green cabbage
½ cup shredded red cabbage
1 stick celery, shredded
½ cup fresh bean sprouts
½ cup grated carrot (moderate)
½ cup grated cheese
3 tablespoons sour cream

For a delicious, easy light lunch, fill pita pockets with lettuce or green cabbage, red cabbage, celery, carrot and bean sprouts. Top with 2 tablespoons of savoury mince, a sprinkle of grated cheese and ½ tablespoon sour cream
or
Line centre of flat bread with ingredients in same order, roll up and serve.

FOR BREAD CASES

Preheat oven to 180C/350F. Butter slices of bread with rice bran spread. Cut round shape from each slice using 3cm/2inch cutter. Push a round into each muffin tray compartment buttered side down till it fits snugly. Bake 10 minutes in till crisp. Take out of oven. Remove from tray and fill with hot mince mixture.

- Meat mixture is also yummy on toast, or as a filling for a toasted sandwich.
- Savoury mince is delicious as a filling for cannelloni tubes, or for lasagna, toped with cheese sauce.

This wonderfully versatile mince recipe can be frozen and used a base for a quick weeknight meal.

SHEPHERD'S PIE

Savoury mince recipe (see page 38)
1 cup frozen peas

Make savoury mince recipe adding frozen peas after meat is cooked with rest of carrot, spring onion, celery etc.

Heat oil in large saucepan. Add garlic, ¼ of parsley, celery, carrot and spring onion and cook till garlic is slightly golden. Add mince and break up with wooden spoon. Continue stirring till meat is cooked. Add frozen peas, rest of carrot, spring onion, celery and garlic with miso and water. Cook all together, stirring from time to time, till liquid has nearly all gone, about 20 minutes. Add brufax. Spread meat mixture into a medium size pyrex baking dish. Spread potato covering over carefully with fork to cover evenly.

POTATO TOPPING

6 medium old season potatoes
2 eggs
2 tablespoons grated tasty cheese, low fat if preferred
Pinch of sea salt

Peel and chop potatoes and boil 20 minutes or so, till soft. Drain well and mash thoroughly with 2 lightly beaten eggs. Add salt and cheese.

Bake in pre-heated oven at 180C/350F for 30 minutes, till topping is crisp and golden.

CHICKEN DRUMSTICKS WITH STUFFING

8 chicken drumsticks
1 cup soft fresh wholemeal breadcrumbs
8 slices bacon
2 spring onions, finely sliced
1 tablespoon finely chopped parsley
1 clove garlic, crushed
3 tablespoons rice bran or canola oil

Preheat oven to 180C/350F.

Heat oil and panfry spring onions and garlic until spring onions are soft. Take off heat and stir in breadcrumbs and parsley.

Lift skin off one side of chicken leg to form a pocket between the skin and the meat. Fill each pocket with stuffing mix. Wrap a piece of bacon around each leg and place wrapped legs on lightly oiled baking tray.

Roast until golden and well cooked, about 30 minutes. Serve with pear sauce (see page 102) or tamarillo chutney (moderate) (see page 100).

These are very good for a picnic.

CHICKEN CASSEROLE

4 chicken legs (leg and thigh pieces)
¼ cup flour
2 tablespoons bran oil

3 cloves garlic, finely chopped
1 tablespoon parsley, finely chopped
½ carrot, peeled and diced (moderate)
2 sticks celery with green top, diced finely
2 slices bacon, finely chopped
2 spring onions, finely diced
3 tablespoons rice bran oil

1 tablespoon miso paste
2 cups hot water
1 tablespoon pear sauce (see page 102) or tamarillo chutney (moderate) (see page 100)
¼ cup brufax (yeast flakes)

2 large old season potatoes cut in serving size pieces
1 parsnip, peeled and cut in serving size pieces (moderate)
1 carrot cut in serving size pieces (moderate)
1 sweet potato cut in serving size pieces (moderate)

1 dessertspoon cornflour mixed with 2 tablespoons water (or whiskey or vodka)

Toss chicken in flour and pan fry in 1 tablespoon heated oil in stove-top to oven pot, till golden, approximately 5 minutes. Remove from pan. Add 2 tablespoon oil and brown bacon and garlic. Add parsley, carrot, celery and spring onions and cook stirring all the time for about 5 minutes to infuse flavours. Add miso paste and hot water and stir well. Return chicken to pot with potatoes, carrot and sweet potato.

Cover and continue to cook on low heat on element for an hour or in oven pre-heated to 180C/350F with the occasional stir, checking contents do not stick and adding more water if necessary. Add chutney and brufax, and thicken casserole sauce with cornflour and water if required. Vodka or whisky can be used to thicken at the end for richer flavour.

Serve sprinkled with a little extra finely chopped parsley. Accompany with two or three triangles of white bread per person, pan fried in rice bran oil and drained on paper towels.

Great with a side salad or fresh steamed green beans or peas.

All or some of moderate sal ingredients can be omitted.

Serves 4

CHICKEN WITH ASIAN VEGETABLES

4 skinless chicken breasts cut in bite sized pieces
3 medium size pak choy (moderate)
2 cloves garlic, peeled and finely chopped
2 sticks celery, finely sliced
20 fresh green beans, tailed, chopped and cut in half
10 snow peas (moderate)
6 Brussels sprouts, halved
¼ small Savoy cabbage, finely shredded
1 cup mung bean sprouts
1 teaspoons soft brown sugar
1 tablespoon mirin (rice wine)
1 tablespoon soy sauce
Rice bran oil for cooking
½ cup raw cashew pieces

Heat oil in large pot or wok. Pan fry chicken with garlic. Add Brussels sprouts and green beans and cook five minutes, stirring.

In small jug mix brown sugar, mirin and soy sauce, add to pot, followed by pak choy, celery, snow peas, savoy cabbage and mung bean sprouts. Toss and cook for five minutes or so till vegetables just cooked but still crunchy.

Serve with steamed rice and top with raw cashew pieces..

Serves 4

ORZO CHICKEN STIR FRY

500gms/1lb chicken mince
1 cup cooked orzo pasta (could use ribbons/penne pasta)
1 tablespoon mirin (rice wine)
1 tablespoon organic Tamari (wheat free soy sauce)
2 teaspoons miso paste
2 teaspoons soft brown sugar
1 large stick celery, finely chopped
3 cloves garlic, peeled and diced
1 tablespoon finely chopped parsley
10 fresh green beans halved or 10 sugar snap peas (moderate)
½ cup chopped raw cashew nuts
Rice bran oil to cook

Heat oil in large frying pan or wok. Add chicken mince and stir till cooked through. Add celery, garlic, parsley and green beans or sugar snap peas. Stir and cook for few minutes. Add mirin, soy sauce, miso paste and brown sugar, combine then add orzo pasta. Cook couple more minutes till orzo is heated through.

Serve in small bowls or large lettuce leaves, sprinkled with chopped raw cashews.

Serves 4

TURKEY TENDERLOINS OR BREASTS, STUFFED

750gms/1 ½ lb turkey breast or tenderloins
   (probably 2 breasts or tenderloins)
4 to 6 slices of bacon

BACON AND RICOTTA STUFFING

15gms/½ oz butter melted
2 slices bacon, finely chopped
1 tablespoon canola oil
3 spring onions, finely chopped
1 clove garlic, crushed
250gms/8ozs ricotta cheese
2 tablespoons finely grated parmesan cheese
1 egg, beaten
1 cup fresh breadcrumbs
¼ cup finely chopped fresh parsley

TO MAKE STUFFING

Remove rind from bacon and chop finely. Heat oil in pan and add bacon, onion and garlic and cook till onion and garlic are soft and bacon is cooked. In a medium sized bowl, put ricotta and parmesan cheeses, egg, breadcrumbs, parsley and spring onions. Add bacon, onion and garlic and mix together lightly to combine ingredients.

Preheat oven to 180C/350F.

One at a time, put tenderloins or breasts between two pieces of cling wrap and flatten till about half their size again using the flat side of a meat cleaver.

Place prepared stuffing down centre of each piece of flattened turkey. Roll up and wrap 2 to 3 slices of bacon round each one. Fasten with wooden toothpick.

Place in greased baking pan with a ½ cup of water. Bake uncovered for an hour, basting 2 or 3 times.

When cooked, remove toothpicks and let rest on kitchen bench for half an hour, before slicing into 1.5cm / ½ inch thick pieces.

Tip: Make a delicious sauce by taking liquid from cooking. Put in small saucepan. Add a dessertspoon of pear sauce (see page 102) or rhubarb jam (moderate) (see page 98), tablespoon of cornflour, dessertspoon of miso and ¼ cup vodka.

Heat till boiling, then simmer a couple of minutes.

PARMESAN CRUSTED FISH

4 x 150 gms/5ozs skinned and boned white fish fillets - a medium to thick fish is best
½ cup finely grated parmesan
2 tablespoons rice bran spread

Pre-heat oven to 180C, fan bake.

Line oven dish with baking paper. Lay slices out flat.

Combine parmesan and rice bran spread and smooth over top of fish fillets. Bake about 20 minutes till fish cooked through, then grill for 2 to 3 minutes, till golden.

Serve with roasted potato slices and steamed fresh green beans.

Use freshly made sal free mayonnaise (see page 102) or tamarillo chutney (moderate) (see page 100) as a condiment.

Serves 4.

FRESH TUNA CAKES

3 or 4 tuna steaks total weight around 750gms/1 ½ lbs
Level tablespoon miso paste
Tablespoon mirin (rice wine)
Tablespoon organic tamari (wheat free soy sauce)

Rice bran oil to pan fry.

Slice each steak through middle. Cut in small cubes. Mix well with miso, mirin and tamari soy sauce. Leave to marinate 30 minutes or so.

Squeeze small handfuls and shape into patties, about 60cms/2 ½ inches round. Pan fry in rice bran oil till cooked to your preference. (Around ten minutes for well cooked). Turn over carefully so patties stay intact. Reduce heat to cook on flipped side.

Serve with pear sauce (see page 102) or tamarillo chutney (moderate) (see page 100). Delicious made as small bite size canapes.

Makes 8 to 10 standard size cakes.

Serves 4 people

WHITE FISH FILO PARCELS

4 x 150 gms/5ozs skinned a boned white fish fillets (Terakihi, Snapper)
1 carrot (moderate and optional)
1 leek
1 dessertspoon butter
125 gms/4ozs soft cream cheese
Pinch salt
8 large sheets filo pastry
2 tablespoons poppy seeds (optional)
Rice Bran oil spray

Cut each fish fillet into 2 equal pieces. Peel and chop carrot into small cubes and finely slice leek. Melt dessertspoon of butter in small saucepan, add carrot and leek and cook for about about 6 or 7 minutes till just soft. Season with salt.

Spray two sheets of filo pastry with rice bran oil. Place one piece of prepared fish, centrally and towards top end of pastry. Spread fish with 1 oz cream cheese and top with quarter of leek and carrot mixture. Fold filo pastry over fish and vegetables from end to end (approx 4 folds) tucking sides underneath the parcel. Repeat for remaining fish pieces. Spray top of parcels and sprinkle with poppy seeds

Place on baking paper in 190C/375F preheated oven and bake for 20 minutes till fish is cooked through and parcel is golden. Serve with crisp iceberg lettuce salad and potato souffle (see page 91).

Serves 4.

RICE, PASTA & EGGS

FRIED RICE

4 cups cold cooked long grain white rice
3 slices finely chopped bacon
1 tablespoon finely chopped parsley
2 eggs
2 or 3 green beans, finely chopped and cooked
½ cup cooked peas
1 stick celery, finely diced
½ cup mung bean sprouts
4 spring onions, finely chopped
2 tablespoons rice bran oil
1 tablespoon soy sauce
1 tablespoon mirin (rice wine)
½ cup raw cashews

Beat eggs lightly, add parsley and a pinch of salt and make omelette in small frying pan. When cool, cut into small squares.

Heat oil in large deep frying pan or wok. Cook bacon and spring onions. Add rice and continuing to stir from time to time, cook on good heat for about 20 minutes till dry and crispy. Add peas, beans, mung bean sprouts, celery, soy sauce and rice wine and combine well. Finally stir in prepared omelette.

Serve sprinkled with ½ cup raw cashews.

Serves 4 to 6

FRITTATA

2 tablespoons canola or rice bran oil
5 or 6 eggs
1 tablespoon finely chopped parsley
2 cloves garlic, finely chopped
2 medium old season potatoes, peeled and cubed and just cooked so still firm
2 slices bacon, finely chopped
1 spring onion, finely diced
4 Brussels sprouts, finely sliced (optional)
6 green beans, strings removed and finely diced (optional)
125gms/4ozs feta cheese, cubed
½ cup grated cheddar cheese
Pinch of sea salt

Pre heat oven to 180C/350F. Heat oil in large skillet or frying pan that is also suitable for oven cooking. Fry bacon, add garlic when nearly cooked, then potatoes. When golden add spring onions, Brussels sprouts, green beans and parsley. Toss and take off heat. Sprinkle over feta, cheddar cheese and pinch of sea salt, then pour over lightly beaten eggs. Reduce heat and cook till starting to set. Place in centre of heated oven and cook till set and golden, about 20 minutes.

Delicious served with a little tamarillo chutney (moderate) (see page 100) or pear sauce (see page 102) on the side and a tossed green salad (see page 64). Great the next day for lunch, either hot or cold. Cut in small pieces, it also makes a great snack with drinks.

Serves 4 - 6

OPEN FACED OMELETTE

6 eggs
125gms/4ozs feta, cubed or crumbled
2 leeks, white part only finely chopped
30gms/1oz butter
Pinch rock salt
Little finely chopped parsley or chives
   to decorate

Heat oven grill.

Melt half the butter in pan, add chopped leaks and cook till softened. Put aside in small dish. Lightly beat eggs and season with salt. Melt remaining butter in pan, add egg mixture and cook two to three minutes till base is starting to firm.

Scatter leeks and feta cheese over top of omelette. Put in oven under grill till eggs are cooked and top is golden. Remove from pan and serve lightly sprinkled with finely chopped parsley or chives.

A perfect dish for breakfast, brunch or lunch. This could also be made in a smaller fry pan as individual omelettes.

Serves 4

PENNE PASTA WITH FRESH GREENS

400gms/14ozs penne pasta
3 tablespoons rice bran oil
1 tablespoon parsley, finely chopped
2 cloves garlic, finely chopped
155gms/5ozs feta cheese
15 fresh young beans steamed till tender but crisp or ½ cup of steamed fresh peas
1 tablespoon finely chopped chives
Pinch of sea salt

Cook penne and drain. While pasta is cooking, heat oil in a medium saucepan, add garlic, parsley, beans or peas and sea salt. Toss through pasta. Serve in pasta bowls sprinkled with feta cheese and chopped chives.

Serves 4

Tip

Replace penne with bow pasta.

Another yummy dish is to simply stir about three tablespoons parsley pesto (see page 22) through the drained penne and add 3 rashers finely chopped, crisply cooked bacon.

PEA RISOTTO

2 cups Arborio rice (risotto rice)
375gms/12ozs frozen baby peas
2 cloves garlic, finely chopped
2 tablespoons finely chopped parsley
60mls/2 fluid ozs rice bran oil
90gms/3ozs butter
2 slices bacon, finely chopped
5 cups hot water
3 tablespoons miso paste
⅓ cup grated tasty cheese or Parmesan cheese
    plus little extra for garnish

In food processor process frozen baby peas with 2 cups hot water to make a puree. Heat pea puree in saucepan with rest of water and miso paste and leave to simmer.

Saute bacon and garlic in rice bran oil and 60gms/2ozs of butter for few minutes till cooked. Add rice and stir well with wooden spoon till rice is translucent. Do not brown.

Add large ladle of hot pea/miso liquid and continue to stir till liquid is fully absorbed. Continue this process, one ladle at a time till grains are tender but still firm, about 20 minutes. Add parsley and cheese, then last of the butter. Stir well. Serve with a little extra finely grated cheese on top.

Serves 6

Use any leftover risotto to make superb risotto cakes at a later date (see page 57).

RISOTTO CAKES

1 cup cold cooked risotto (pea risotto works beautifully) (see page 56)
½ cup flour
2 tablespoons canola oil
Cubes of feta cheese

Form risotto into balls and flatten into patties.

Push a cube of feta into each patty. Dust with flour.

Heat oil in frying pan and cook a few minutes on each side till crisp and golden.

Serve with tamarillo chutney (moderate) (see page 100) and a tossed salad (see page 64).

RICE PAPER SPRING ROLLS

8 rice paper sheet wrappers
8 large cooked prawns, peeled, deveined and sliced in half, or
1 cup cooked diced white chicken breast, or
1 small cooked pork fillet finely sliced, or
Cup of cubed tofu pan fired in little rice bran oil for few minutes

⅓ cup celery, finely diced
⅓ cup bean sprouts
2 spring onions, finely sliced
⅓ cup finely sliced (julienne) of carrots (moderate)
1 tablespoon finely chopped coriander (moderate)
8 snow or sugar snap peas (moderate)
1 tablespoon finely chopped parsley
1 cup finely chopped iceberg lettuce
1 tablespoon finely chopped cashews

Cooked rice noodles

If using moderate ingredients, blanch snow peas/sugar snap peas and carrots by covering with boiling water, leaving 2 to 3 minutes, then draining and plunging in ice cold water, then draining again.

Dip each rice paper wrapper in water for a few seconds until soft. Put wrapper on tea towel on flat surface and place a line of iceberg lettuce down middle leaving about 5cms clear on each side. Top with sprouts, spring onions, snow or sugar snap peas (optional), carrots (optional), coriander (optional) and parsley. Finish with prawns or chicken, pork or tofu sprinkled with chopped cashews. Fold in uncovered wrapper sides, then roll tightly to enclose filling. Repeat for rest of wrappers.

(You can also add a little of the cooked rice noodles to the filling or finely sliced celery or replace lettuce with finely chopped cabbage).

DIPPING SAUCE

1 tablespoon spoon miso melted in a cup of water.

You can also add teaspoon soy sauce, a teaspoon maple syrup and 1 clove crushed garlic, to miso liquid if you like or 1 tablespoon cashew nut maple butter (see page 104)

Serve with rice noodles.

It is great fun to put each ingredient in separate small bowls and let everyone make their own rice paper spring rolls.

SAFFRON RICE

1 cup basmati rice
2 cups chicken stock (see page 105)
1 ½ tablespoons rice bran or canola oil
3 spring onions, finely sliced
1 clove garlic crushed
½ teaspoon rock salt
½ teaspoon saffron, crumbled
½ tablespoon finely chopped parsley

Heat oil in medium saucepan with a lid.

Add spring onions and garlic and cook gently for 5 minutes till soft. Add rice and stir for 2 to 3 minutes till coated with oil mixture. Add chicken stock, rock salt, saffron and parsley. Bring to boil. Reduce heat and cover.

Simmer for 15 minutes or so till liquid is absorbed.

Fluff up with fork before serving.

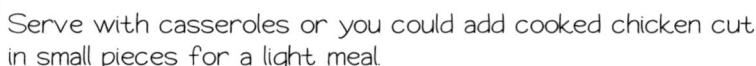

Serve with casseroles or you could add cooked chicken cut in small pieces for a light meal.

SALADS & VEGETABLES

CAESAR SALAD

1 iceberg lettuce
⅓ cup finely grated parmesan cheese
1 stalk celery, finely diced
3 eggs boiled, peeled and cut into quarters or mashed roughly with a fork
4 rashers bacon, diced and cooked till crisp
2 toast thick slices rye, wholemeal or white bread made into croutons
½ cup salad dressing (see page 103)

Prepare lettuce by tearing into pieces, rinsing and drying gently with paper towels. Place on attractive platter. Sprinkle with celery, cheese, egg, bacon and croutons. Drizzle over dressing.

To make croutons, cut off crusts, then cut each slice into 12 or 16 cubes. Panfry in hot rice bran oil till golden. Drain on paper towel.

Serves 4

Tip

Grilled chicken breast, cut into small pieces makes a yummy addition.

Combine vinegar and oil dressing with a tablespoon of mayonnaise for a creamy dressing.

COLE SLAW

½ small green cabbage
¼ small red cabbage
4 stalks celery
1 tablespoon finely chopped parsley
4 spring onions
1 small carrot (moderate)
125mls / ½ cup of salad dressing (see page 103)
  or mayonnaise (see page 102)
Pinch of salt

Wash vegetables.

Shred green and red cabbage, slice spring onions and celery finely. Grate carrot.

Put prepared vegetables in bowl. Toss together with chopped parsley and pinch of salt.

Toss in vinegar and oil dressing or mayonnaise.

Add peeled and finely chopped yellow skinned apple, like golden delicious (moderate) just before serving.

FRESH GREEN AND RED SALAD

1 iceberg lettuce,
1 stick celery
½ cup fresh cooked peas cooled
½ cup finely sliced red cabbage
½ cup of lentil or pea sprouts
2 toast thick slices rye, wholemeal or white bread made into croutons (optional)
¼ cup raw cashew pieces (optional)

Wash iceberg lettuce leaves and tear into small pieces. Slice celery finely. Arrange lettuce pieces on attractive serving dish.

Sprinkle with peas, celery, red cabbage, lentil or pea sprouts and croutons or cashews.

Drizzle with vinegar and oil salad dressing (see page 103).

To make croutons, cut off crusts, then cut each slice into 12 or 16 cubes. Panfry in hot rice bran oil till golden. Drain on paper towel.

LARB - THAI MEAT SALAD

500 gms/1 lb meat mince - chicken, beef, pork or turkey
2 tablespoons jasmine rice
2 tablespoons rice bran oil
½ teaspoon citric acid stirred into 2 tablespoons malt vinegar
1 teaspoon brown sugar
⅓ cup chopped coriander leaves (moderate)
3 finely sliced spring onions
1 stick of celery finely diced
4 cloves garlic finely chopped
⅓ cup raw cashew nuts finely chopped
1 iceberg lettuce

In dry large frying pan or wok, cook rice until golden brown. Remove and crush in mortar and pestle or in small food processor till finely ground.

In large frying pan or wok, heat rice bran oil and fry garlic till crisp and golden. Add meat to pan and cook with garlic, about 5 minutes till cooked through, breaking mince up with wooden spoon. Remove from pan. Add sugar, citric acid mix, spring onions, celery, crushed rice, raw cashew nuts, cooked garlic and coriander if using this. Put in separate bowl and let cool. Add mince mixture to liquid ingredients. Lightly stir together and place generous mound in separate lettuce leaves. Makes about 8.

A quantity of rice can be prepared in advance and stored in an air tight jar. Alternatively this mixture can be used in rice paper spring rolls recipe (see page 58).

POTATO SALAD

6 old season potatoes, peeled and boiled till firm but cooked.
2 spring onions finely sliced
1 stick celery, finely diced
2 hard boiled eggs, thickly sliced (optional)
½ cup mayonnaise (see page 102)
1 tablespoon finely chopped chives

Cut potato into cubes and while still warm, combine with other ingredients.

Serve with finely chopped chives sprinkled on top.

SALAD LYONNAISE

1 iceberg lettuce
1 stick celery, finely diced
1 thick slice ham, chopped in small pieces
½ cup finely chopped gouda or gruyere cheese
1 egg, boiled and mashed with a fork

Wash iceberg lettuce leaves and tear into small pieces. Slice celery finely.

If serving as a side salad, arrange lettuce pieces on large attractive serving dish. As a lunch or entree, use small deep round individual dishes.

Sprinkle lettuce with celery, ham and cheese and finally mashed egg. Drizzle with vinegar and oil salad dressing (see page 103)

Serves 4.

TUNA SALAD

1 iceberg lettuce
10 green beans, steamed few minutes (crisp but tender)
1 spring onion, finely sliced
2 old season potatoes, peeled, cubed and boiled till just tender
1 tin tuna chunks in spring water (medium or large tin)
6 anchovies (optional)
3 eggs, hard boiled, peeled and cut in quarters
½ cup dressing (see page 103)

Place clean lettuce leaves on base of platter.

Scatter over beans, potato cubes, tuna chunks, eggs and anchovies. Finish with spring onion.

Drizzle with dressing. Excellent for lunch or as a summer starter.

Serves 4

Tuna could be replaced with peeled and de-veined prawns or fresh chunks of crayfish for a special treat.

WARM PUMPKIN, GREEN BEAN AND FETA SALAD

374gms/12ozs dry pumpkin, butternut or squash (moderate)
1 ½ tablespoons rice bran oil
3 rashers bacon cut into small pieces
20 tender young green beans steamed till just tender
10 snow peas, blanched in hot then cold water (moderate)
125gms feta, cubed
⅓ cup raw cashew pieces or ½ cup mung bean sprouts (moderate) (optional)
Rice bran oil spray
⅓ cup vinegar and oil dressing (see page 103)

Pre-heat oven to 180C/350F.

Peel pumpkin, butternut or squash and cube. Place on oven tray and spray with rice bran oil. Cook in oven about 15 minutes till cooked but firm.

Heat rice bran oil in frying pan, add bacon and cook till just crisp. Place pumpkin, butternut or squash on platter, sprinkle over beans, snow peas, feta, bacon and cashew pieces and/or mung bean sprouts if you like.

Drizzle over dressing.

MASHED SWEET POTATO

¾ kilo/1 ½ lbs sweet potato or traditional red
    skinned kumera (moderate)
125gms/4ozs butter or rice bran spread
2 level tablespoons miso

Peel sweet potato and cut into even pieces
2 to 3 cms/1in. Boil till soft.

Drain well, then mash thoroughly with butter
or rice bran spread and miso.

Keep in covered dish in oven on low heat till ready
to serve.

POTATO SOUFFLE

6 large old season potatoes
4 eggs
Rounded tablespoon butter or rice bran oil spread
Pinch of sea salt

Peel and chop potatoes. Boil till soft.

Separate eggs. Whip whites till stiff. Lightly whip yolks. Mash hot potatoes with butter, salt and egg yolks. When mixture is creamy, fold in beaten egg whites.

Empty into a buttered 18cm/7ins round souffle dish. Bake in preheated oven 180C/350F for 30 minutes till golden brown.

Can be prepared in advance earlier in day and kept in fridge, till ready to cook. Prepared potato mix can be put in 4 to 6 individual souffle dishes and cooked at same heat for approximately 20 minutes.

TASTY LENTILS

1 cup dry brown lentils
4 cups boiling water
1 small carrot, finely cubed (moderate)
1 stick celery, finely chopped
2 slices bacon, finely chopped or thick slice ham, finely cubed
1 clove garlic, finely chopped
2 tablespoons rice bran oil
4-5 dessertspoons plain unsweetened yoghurt
Little extra chopped garlic

Pan fry carrot, celery, bacon or ham, and garlic couple of minutes to infuse flavours. Add lentils and boiling water. Stir well, cover and simmer half hour or so till liquid has evaporated and lentils are soft.

Delicious topped with plain unsweetened yoghurt and a little chopped garlic.

A great lunch dish by itself or side dish with meat or fish. Carrot can be omitted or just a little used for flavour.

Serves 4 to 6

VEGETABLES – GREEN & ROOT

Low in salicylates, or moderate as marked

GREEN VEGETABLES

Serve raw or cooked by blanching, steaming, tossing in a wok or stir frying in a pan:

Asparagus (moderate)

Bamboo shoots

Brussels sprouts

Cabbage green (and red)

Celery

Chinese vegetables – Bok Choy and Chinese cabbage (both moderate)

Chives

Green beans

Green peas

Leek

Lettuce – Iceberg

Lettuce – other (moderate)

Marrow (moderate)

Mung bean sprouts

Snow peas and sprouts (moderate)

Spring onions (no round bulb – look like small leeks)

ROOT VEGETABLES

Serve baked crisp in oil, or steamed or boiled, then tossed in hot butter or mashed with a little sour cream, salt and butter. Roast individually or a combination served hot or cold tossed in a yummy mayonnaise or dressing (see pages 102, 103):

Beetroot (moderate)

Carrot – cooked or raw (moderate)

Parsnip (moderate)

Potato without skin – old season preferable

Pumpkin (moderate)

Sweet potato or Kumera (moderate)

Turnip (moderate)

BAKING

BANANA CAKE

125gms/4ozs butter
185gms/6ozs sugar
2 eggs
2-3 ripe bananas, mashed
1 teaspoon vanilla essence
1 teaspoon baking soda
2 tablespoons warm milk
1 teaspoon baking powder
250gms/8ozs flour

Preheat oven to 180C/350F. Grease a loose-bottom 20cms/8ins cake tin and line with baking paper.

Cut butter into small pieces and place in bowl with sugar. Beat till creamy. Add eggs one at a time, beating thoroughly each time. Add mashed bananas. Dissolve baking soda in warm milk and add to mixture. Gradually stir in sifted flour and baking powder. Pour into prepared cake tin. Bake in preheated oven for 45 minutes till wooden skewer comes out clean. Ice with vanilla icing if you like.

VANILLA ICING

50 gms butter
2 cups icing sugar
2 teaspoons vanilla essence
2 tablespoons milk

Cut butter in small pieces and beat butter till creamy. Add icing sugar, vanilla essence and milk and beat till light and fluffy. Spread over cooled cake.

Instead of icing, cake can be topped with 85gms/3ozs butter, ½ cup soft brown sugar, 1 tablespoon flour, rubbed together and sprinkled over top of cake before baking.

CHOCOLATE CARAMEL SQUARES

BISCUIT BASE

2/3 cup flour
1 teaspoon baking powder
2 tablespoons soft brown sugar
75gms/3ozs butter

Preheat oven to 180C/350F.

Grease 18cms x 28cms/7ins x 11ins baking tin and line with baking paper. Put sifted flour, baking powder in a bowl with sugar and butter. Mix by rubbing with your fingers until a crumbly loose dough is formed.

Press mixture firmly into baking tin to form a solid base. Cook in preheated oven for 15 minutes.

FILLING

2 x 395gms/12.5oz tins sweetened condensed milk
1/3 cup golden syrup
50gms/1¾ ozs butter

Place condensed milk, golden syrup and butter in a saucepan and stir over low heat for about 15 minutes, until golden brown.

Pour filling evenly over warm biscuit base and return to oven for 10 minutes.

Remove and leave to cool for 15 minutes, then refrigerate.

TOPPING

125gms/7ozs (approx) dark chocolate.

Use 70% cocoa dark chocolate for a more healthy, luscious chocolate tasting result.

50gms/1¾ ozs butter

Combine chopped chocolate and butter in heatproof bowl and place over pan of simmering hot water. Do not let bowl or contents touch water.

Stir until melted and smooth. Pour chocolate mixture over filling, tapping tin on bench till topping is evenly spread.

Leave to set, then remove from tin and cut into squares.

Most recipes for chocolate caramel squares use coconut in the base, which is a high salicylate.

This delicious version, doesn't.

CHOCOLATE COOKIES

125 gms/4 ½ ozs softened butter or rice bran spread
¾ cup fine brown sugar
2 teaspoons real vanilla essence
1 ½ cups plain flour
1 rounded teaspoon baking powder
¾ cup of 70% cocoa dark chocolate, or white chocolate broken into small pieces or white chocolate buttons broken into halves, or a combination of dark and white chocolate
⅓ cup rice bran oil

Preheat oven to 180C/350F fan bake.

Beat butter or rice bran spread and sugar in a medium bowl till pale and creamy. Add vanilla essence and beat till combined. Add flour and baking powder and beat till crumbly. Add enough extra rice bran oil to make mixture stick together. Stir in chosen chocolate.

Mould into walnut size balls, rolling between palms of the hands till smooth and round.

Place on 2 large oven trays lined with baking paper. Flatten each ball gently with a fork till about 3 to 4cms/1 to 1 ½ ins across.

Bake till just golden for 15 minutes or a little more. Leave to rest for a few minutes then cool on wire rack.

Makes about 20.

FRUIT MUFFINS

2 cups flour
1 tablespoon baking powder
3 tablespoons sugar
1 cup milk
50mls canola oil
1 egg, beaten
1 cup fruit
Either pear tinned (in sugar syrup),
         drained and chopped
    or fresh pear, peeled and chopped
    or mashed banana
    or cooked pieces of rhubarb (moderate)
    or peeled, grated, yellow skinned apple
         (moderate)
    or cubes of fresh or tinned mango
         (moderate)

Preheat oven to 200C/400F.

Combine flour, baking powder and sugar. Add beaten egg to milk and oil. Stir this liquid into flour combination. Add fruit of choice and mix lightly, just to combine.

Grease a 12 serving medium size muffin tin and ¾ fill each cup. Bake 15 to 20 minutes till wooden skewer poked in centre of a muffin comes out clean.

Sprinkle each muffin with a little sugar or add ½ a teaspoon of cream cheese to centre of each muffin, before baking.

MUESLI BARS

1 cup flour
1 ½ teaspoons baking powder
½ cup fine brown sugar
1 ½ tablespoons golden syrup
2 cups rolled oats
½ cup fine bran flakes
1 cup chocolate drops
155gms/5ozs butter or rice bran spread
1 tablespoon canola oil

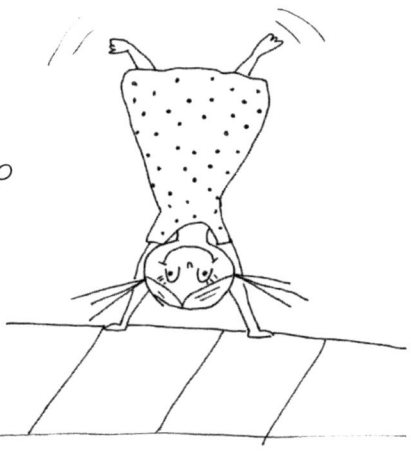

Preheat oven to 180C/350F.

Mix flour, baking powder, oats, bran and brown sugar in a large bowl. Melt butter and combine with oil and golden syrup. Add to dry ingredients. Finely mix in chocolate drops.

Press mixture into a medium size slice tray with a removable bottom, which as been greased and lined with baking paper.

Bake 20 to 25 minutes until golden.

Cut into bars while still hot but leave to cool before removing from tray. Store in air tight tin, if you can keep some!

PEAR CAKE

3 pears, peeled and finely sliced
1 cup caster sugar
1 ½ cups flour
Pinch of salt
1 teaspoon baking powder
1 teaspoon baking soda
125gms/4ozs butter melted
1 egg
1 teaspoon pure vanilla essence
Icing sugar to decorate

Preheat oven to 180C/350F.

Combine pears and caster sugar.

In a separate bowl, sift flour, salt, baking powder and baking soda.

Combine melted butter, vanilla essence and lightly beaten egg with pear and sugar mixture.

Bake in medium size cake tin about 40 - 50 minutes. (Works very well in a ring tin). Test with wooden skewer.

Sprinkle with icing sugar when cool

POPPY SEED CUPCAKES

¼ cup poppy seeds
½ cup plain yoghurt
½ cup white sugar
½ cup soft butter
2 eggs
1 ¼ cups flour
½ teaspoon baking soda
1 teaspoon baking powder

Preheat oven to 180C/350C.

Fill each cup of a 12 medium-size muffin tray with paper cups. Stir poppy seeds into yoghurt in a small container and leave while preparing rest of mixture.

In a medium bowl beat together butter, sugar and eggs for 5 minutes or so, till thick and creamy.

Sift together flour, baking soda and baking powder and beat this in two or three lots into butter/sugar/egg mixture, alternating with yoghurt and poppy seed combination, till just combined and smooth. Don't over beat.

⅔rds fill each paper cup and bake for 25 minutes till lightly brown and a wooden skewer poked in centre of a muffin, comes out clean.

Makes 12

Fabulous with citric icing and topped with a whole cashew nut or sprinkle of poppy seeds. For icing combine ⅔ cup of icing sugar and ½ teaspoon citric acid with just enough water to make thick paste. Top each muffin with icing and add a whole cashew to decorate.

POPPY SEED LOAF

¼ cup butter softened
1 cup soft brown sugar, firmly packed
2 teaspoons natural vanilla essence
1 egg
2 cups flour
1 teaspoon baking soda
2 teaspoons baking powder
Pinch salt
1 cup buttermilk
3 tablespoons poppy seeds

Preheat oven to 180C/350C.

Grease and line with baking powder a 23x12.5/7.5cms or 9x5x3ins loaf pan

Cream butter and sugar then stir in lightly beaten egg and vanilla essence.

Sift flour, baking soda, baking powder together and add poppy seeds and salt to dry ingredients. Alternate adding the flour mixture and buttermilk to creamed mixture (half of each at a time) stirring till just blended.

Pour batter into prepared loaf pan. Bake just over an hour, till lightly golden and a wooden skewer poked in the middle of the loaf comes out clean. Cool in pan.

Tip

If you don't have any buttermilk, substitute with 1 cup of plain yoghurt (if very thick, use ½ milk and ½ plain yoghurt) or 1 cup milk to which you add one rounded teaspoon cream of tartar.

RHUBARB & APPLE CAKE
(Rhubarb & apple are moderate)

60gms/2ozs butter softened
1 ½ cups soft brown sugar
2 eggs
1 teaspoon pure vanilla extract
300gms/10.5ozs flour
300gms/10.5ozs rhubarb (moderate) in
    2 cms/½ in pieces
2 yellow skinned apples like Golden Delicious
    (moderate), peeled and chopped into small pieces
1 teaspoon baking soda
1 teaspoon salt
1 cup sour cream or plain yoghurt

CAKE TOPPING

¼ cup white sugar

Preheat oven to 160C/325F fan bake. Grease and line with baking paper a 22 to 24cms/8½ to 9½ ins round cake tin.

Beat butter and brown sugar together. Add eggs one at a time, then vanilla, continuing to beat. Stir in sifted flour, baking soda and salt. Add prepared rhubarb and apple then sour cream or yoghurt and stir till well combined.

Spoon into prepared cake tin. Sprinkle sugar on top of cake. Bake in preheated oven for 1 hr 10mins. Cover with foil after 45 minutes to prevent top becoming too brown. Check if cooked with wooden skewer inserted down middle of cake. Serve with yoghurt, whipped cream or pouring custard.

Keep in fridge as this is a very moist cake with full fruit flavour. Can be eaten cold or slightly warmed in microwave.

DAMPER
(to serve with soup)

2 cups flour
3 teaspoons baking powder
½ teaspoon sea salt
250mls/8 fluid ozs milk

Preheat oven to 200C/400F.

Sift flour, baking powder and salt into mixing bowl. Pour in milk and mix with a knife to form a dough. Turn onto a floured surface and form into a rounded bun about 23cm/9ins in width. Mark into 4 or 6 sections and bake on greased tray for 35 to 30 minutes. Break into sections and serve with butter.

For a tasty addition, add ½ cup of tasty grated cheese before the milk

LITTLE CHEESE MUFFINS

2 cups flour
2 teaspoons baking powder
1 cup milk
2 cups grated cheese
½ teaspoon salt
2 eggs
6 teaspoons cream cheese or tamarillo chutney/3 slices ham or 3 - 6 slices smoked salmon

Preheat oven to 210C/410F. Grease 12 serving size mini muffin pan.

Mix flour, baking powder, salt and cheese. Add lightly beaten eggs and milk. Mix lightly till just blended. Do not over mix.

Three-quarter fill each muffin cup. Cook for 15 minutes till golden. Cut almost in half and tuck ½ a teaspoon cream cheese and/or smoked salmon or tamarillo chutney (moderate) (see page 100) with a small slice of ham.

Lovely for a light lunch or as finger food with drinks.

SAVOURY DROP SCONES

2 cups flour
2 teaspoons baking powder
1 teaspoon salt
1 cup grated cheese
2 finely chopped tablespoons parsley
¾ cup milk
⅓ cup canola oil

Preheat oven to 200C/400F.

Sift flour and baking powder into large bowl, add salt. Add cheese and parsley. Stir in oil and milk till combined into a dough.

Drop tablespoon amounts well spaced, on to a baking tray lined with baking paper.

Cook 15 minutes until golden and skewer poked into centre comes out clean.

DESSERTS

BANANA SOFT-FREEZE ICECREAM

2 ripe bananas
½ cup buttermilk
1 teaspoon pure vanilla essence

Slice bananas into thin rounds and place in a sealed plastic container in the freezer till frozen (at least two hours).

Place frozen slices in strong processor or blender with buttermilk and vanilla essence. Process till creamy.

Serves 2

Simple and totally delicious. You could also fold crushed meringues or chopped chocolate before serving.

COFFEE ICECREAM

2 eggs, separated
60gms/2ozs sieved icing sugar (confectioner
   or powdered sugar)
2 teaspoons instant decaf coffee powder
   melted in 2 tablespoons warm water
150mls/5 fluid ozs cream

Whisk egg whites until very stiff. Gradually whisk in icing sugar.

Whisk egg yolks with coffee and water mix and gradually whisk into egg white and icing sugar combination.

Lightly whip cream and fold into mixture. Pour into shallow tray and freeze. No further beating is needed.

Take out a few minutes before serving to make easier to use.

MAPLE ICECREAM

3 whole eggs
2 extra egg yolks
1 teaspoon pure vanilla extract
2 cups cream
1 cup soft brown sugar, lightly packed
1 cup pure maple syrup

Combine eggs and two extra yolks with vanilla and sugar in a heatproof bowl. Place over a saucepan of simmering water. Beat with a hand-held electric mixer for 7 or 8 minutes until thick.

Take off heat and cool 10 minutes.

Whisk cream until stiff peaks form and fold gently into egg mixture until well combined. Add maple syrup and stir through. Pour into 2 litre/4 cup/3 ½ pint metal tin and cover with foil. Freeze overnight.

Take out 10 minutes before serving to allow icecream to soften a little for easier handling

MINI UPSIDE DOWN PEAR CAKES

1 cup maple syrup
2 pears, peeled, cored and cut into 12 wedge slices
½ cup fine brown sugar
1 cup flour
2 teaspoons of baking powder
1 teaspoon pure vanilla essence
3 large eggs
125gms/4ozs melted butter

Preheat oven to 180C/350F.

Grease 6 ¾ cup size ramekin dishes. Pour equal amounts of maple syrup into each dish. Place 4 slices in a single layer over syrup.

Beat sugar, eggs and vanilla essence until thick and creamy. Fold in sifted flour and baking powder. Stir in melted butter.

Spoon creamed mixture into each prepared ramekin.

Bake in oven for about 20 minutes until golden and cooked through when poked with a wooden skewer.

Sit for a few minutes then invert onto individual serving plates. Serve warm with icecream or custard.

Serves 6

PEAR AND CARAMEL CAKE

CAKE
1 cup soft brown sugar, firmly packed
½ cup rice bran oil
1 tablespoon pure vanilla extract
2 eggs
¼ cup milk
410gms/13ozs(approx) tin pear halves drained and chopped into small pieces
1¾ cups flour
1 level tablespoon baking powder
Pinch salt

Preheat oven to 175C/350F fan bake. Grease and line with baking paper at 23cms/9ins square cake tin.

Put brown sugar, oil, vanilla in a bowl and beat with electric mixer till blended. Add eggs, one at a time, beating well each time. Mix in milk, flour, baking powder and salt and beat a little till blended. Stir in pieces of pear.

Pour mixture into prepared cake tin. Bake in pre-heated oven for around 35 minutes till wooden skewer poked in middle of cake comes out clean. When cooked, remove from oven and poke top of hot cake with wooden skewer all over. Slowly and carefully, pour over hot caramel topping till soaked in. Remove from tin. Serve warm with yoghurt, whipped cream or pure vanilla icecream.

CARAMEL TOPPING

½ cup soft brown sugar, firmly packed
¼ cup butter
¼ cup full cream
1 teaspoon pure vanilla extract

Put brown sugar, butter and cream in a saucepan.

Bring to boil over medium heat. Reduce heat and simmer, stirring for 5 minutes.

Remove from heat and stir in vanilla.

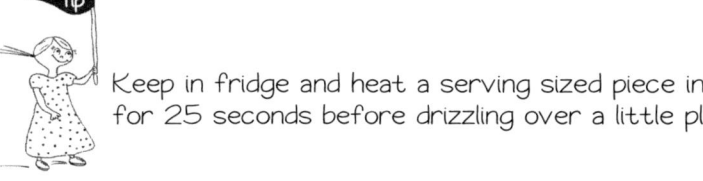

Keep in fridge and heat a serving sized piece in microwave for 25 seconds before drizzling over a little plain yoghurt.

PEAR AND RHUBARB CRUMBLE

Rhubarb is moderate

4 cups chopped fruit - 3 cups chopped pears/1 cup chopped rhubarb (more or less of each according to your preference

½ cup fine brown sugar

CRUMBLE

¾ cup fine brown sugar
¾ cup flour
¾ cup rolled oats
100gms/3 ½ ozs rice bran spread or butter

Preheat oven to 180C/350F.

Simmer fruit with ½ cup brown sugar till tender, about 15 minutes. Share amongst four greased ramekin dishes.

Combine crumble ingredients and form to a crumble with your fingers. Spread over fruit and bake till golden about 20 minutes.

Serve with custard sauce and whipped cream or vanilla icecream.

You could just use pears and add a teaspoon of vanilla essence to have a sal free dish.

JAMS & CHUTNEYS

RHUBARB JAM
Rhubarb is moderate

800gms/1lb 12ozs fresh rhubarb (moderate) cut in small pieces
800gms/1lb 12ozs sugar
½ teaspoon citric acid

Put sugar and fruit in large preserving pan. Stir over low heat with wooden spoon to prevent fruit mixture from sticking. When sugar is completely dissolved, turn up heat. Add citric acid.

Allow jam to boil, stirring from time to time until a little placed on a cold saucer starts to set.

Pour into sterilised jars and seal.

Makes about 3 jars

You can add one peeled, cored and chopped pear with rhubarb and a teaspoon of pure vanilla essence for a slightly different flavour.

RHUBARB RELISH
Rhubarb is moderate

5 cups finely chopped rhubarb (moderate)
¾ cup finely chopped shallots
1 peeled, cored and finely chopped pear
3 ½ cups malt vinegar
2 ½ teaspoons salt
5 cups fine brown sugar
1 teaspoon citric acid melted in teaspoon water

Combine all ingredients in large preserving pan.

Cook over medium heat, stirring with wooden spoon from time to time for about half an hour until mixture has thickened.

Pour into sterilised jars and seal.

Best to keep in fridge.

Makes about 3 to 4 jars.

Delicious with fish and meat.

TAMARILLO CHUTNEY
Tamarillo or tree tomato is moderate

3 kgs/6 ½ lbs tamarillos (34 large size approx) (moderate)
6 - 8 spring onions
4 cups malt vinegar
1 kg/2lbs brown sugar
1 tablespoon salt
½ teaspoon citric acid

Blanch and peel tamarillos, then chop into small pieces. Finely chop white part of spring onions. Put fruit and spring onions in large pot. Add malt vinegar, brown sugar, salt and citric acid. Bring to boil, stirring with wooden spoon.

Reduce heat till at low boil and cook for 1 ½ to 2 hours, stirring from time to time.

Put small spoonful on cold plate and when it gels lightly it is ready. Remove from heat and pour into hot sterilised jars. Seal.

Makes 7½ jars.

Freeze tamarillos when in season and less expensive, to make chutney when you need it.

DRESSINGS, SAUCES, SPREADS & STOCK

MAYONNAISE

1 large egg
½ teaspoon sea salt
½ teaspoon citric acid
1 cup canola oil

Put egg, sea salt and citric acid in food processor or blender. Process or blend till creamy. With machine still running drizzle oil into egg mixture very gradually till all used up. Makes enough to fill a medium jam jar. Keep in fridge. Perfect as a dip or dressing and ideal for potato salad (see page 66)

SAVOURY PEAR SAUCE

410gms/13ozs tin pears in syrup
1 teaspoon citric acid
½ teaspoon sea salt
¼ cup fine brown sugar

Remove pears from syrup. Put syrup in small saucepan and boil about 10 minutes till half the amount. Chop pears very fine and add to syrup with brown sugar, citric acid and salt. Cook on medium heat for another fifteen minutes till thick. Puree and store in fridge. Makes enough to fill a medium size jam jar. A great tasty savoury sauce with any sort of meat or fish.

VINEGAR AND OIL SALAD DRESSING

½ cup rice bran or canola oil
¼ cup malt vinegar
1 ½ tablespoons brown sugar
1 clove fresh garlic, crushed
Generous pinch rock salt
1 tablespoon finely chopped parsley

Blend all ingredients in small food processor or use a hand held bar mix, till well combined and creamy. This can be used as a salad dressing or as a dip for vegetable sticks.

VINEGAR, SOY SAUCE AND OIL DRESSING

Splash maple syrup
¼ cup malt vinegar
½ cup rice bran or canola oil
1 clove fresh garlic, crushed
1 tablespoon soy sauce

Blend all ingredients in small food processor or use a hand held bar mix, till well combined and creamy. All ingredients can also be put in a firmly closed screw top jar and shaken till well combined. Delicious as a dressing for a green or mixed vegetable salad.

CASHEW NUT MAPLE BUTTER

1 cup raw cashews
30mls/1 fluid oz maple syrup
40gms/1 ½ ozs rice bran spread

In food processor, process cashews until finely chopped. With processor still running, make a paste by adding spread and maple syrup. Makes enough to fill one medium jam jar. Keep in fridge. Great on rye toast for breakfast.

CHICKEN STOCK

12 cups water
4 Brussels sprouts, halved
2 sticks celery
½ leek
½ carrot (moderate/optional)
½ parsnip (moderate/optional)
2 sprigs parsley
2 cloves garlic
Bones of one chicken and a ½ cup of chicken meat (cooked or uncooked)
Rock salt

Put Brussels sprouts and roughly chopped celery, leek, carrot, parsnip, parsley and garlic in large pot. Add chicken bones, chicken and salt, then cover with the water and bring to the boil. Simmer 1 ½ hours. Strain.

Stock can be used for soup (see page 30) or frozen in ice cube trays or small containers for use in casseroles or sauces.

SUBSTITUTES & TIPS

SUBSTITUTES

- Peanut butter – Cashew spread
- Lemon – Citric acid
- Coffee – Decaf coffee
- Cider/white/balsamic/ vinegar – Malt vinegar
- Olive oil – Rice bran/safflower/sunflower/canola/soy oils
- Honey – Maple syrup or golden syrup
- Stock – Miso
- Tumeric – Saffron

TIPS

- Pan fry small cubes carrot/celery/bacon/parsley/garlic for tomato based dishes
- Make a pesto with parsley/raw cashews/parmesan/bran oil instead of basil or coriander based pestos.
- Eat rye, wheatmeal or white bread instead of seed and grain varieties
- Steep a vanilla bean in boiling water or add ½ teaspoon pure vanilla essence to hot water instead of herb or green tea
- Use Brufax to flavour and lightly thicken casseroles instead of instant savoury sauce sachets
- When it comes to alcohol you can only drink plain vodka, whiskey or gin.

GENERAL

These recipes use New Zealand measurements

　1 cup = 250 ml

　1 tablespoon = 15 ml

　1 dessertspoon = 2 teaspoons

　1 teaspoon = 5 ml

Both imperial and metric measurements are given where possible.

All ovens are different, so you may need to adjust your cooking temperature or use fan-bake if you prefer.

Moderate ingredients in most dishes are optional expect if it's a main ingredient. Moderate foods are identified in relevant recipes e.g. rhubarb and apple cake.

Provided it does not contain antioxidants, any of the following oils can be used - Canola, safflower, sunflower, soy and rice bran.

I always use free-range nitrite free bacon.

INDEX

B
Baked eggs in individual dishes.............6
Bananas
    banana cake...76
    banana soft freeze icecream..........90
Banana soft freeze icecream..............90
Beef
    beef balls..37
    beef casserole............................34, 35
    shepherd's pie....................................40
Beef casserole....................................34, 35
Bircher muesli..7
Biscuits & slices
    chocolate caramel squares......77, 78
    chocolate cookies..............................79
    muesli bars..81
Breakfast options
Breakfast fruit, yoghurt
    and maple syrup..................................8
Breakfasts
    baked eggs in individual dishes...........6
    breakfast options.................................4
    bircher muesli......................................7
    breakfast fruit, yoghurt
    and maple syrup..................................8
    croque monsieur (toasted bread
    with cheese, ham etc).........................9
    French toast......................................10
    hash browns.......................................11
    pancakes..12
    waffles..13

C
Cakes
    banana cake......................................76
    pear cake...82
    poppy seed cupcakes......................83
    poppy seed loaf................................84
    rhubarb & apple cake..............85, 86
Cashew nut maple butter....................104
Caesar salad...62

Chicken
    chicken balls (or meat balls)............37
    chicken casserole.....................42, 43
    chicken drumsticks with stuffing...41
    chicken with Asian vegetables......44
    orzo chicken stir fry........................45
Chicken balls..37
Chicken casserole...........................42, 43
Chicken drumsticks with stuffing.....41
Chicken soup...30
Chicken stock......................................105
Chicken with Asian vegetables.........44
Chocolate
    chocolate caramel squares......77, 78
    chocolate cookies.............................79
Chocolate caramel squares..........77, 78
Chocolate cookies................................79
Chutney, tamarillo..............................100
Coffee icecream....................................91
Cole slaw..63
Crepe fillings..................................17, 18
Crepes..16
Croque Monsieur (toasted bread
    with cheese, ham etc)........................9

D
Damper...86
Desserts
    banana soft freeze icecream.........90
    coffee icecream.................................91
    maple icecream.................................92
    mini upside down pear cakes.........93
    pear & caramel cake................94, 95
    pear & rhubarb crumble..................96
Dressings & sauces
    mayonnaise......................................102
    savoury pear sauce........................102
    vinegar & oil salad dressing...........103
    vinegar, soy sauce & oil dressing..103

E
Eggs
- baked eggs in individual dishes 6
- frittata 53
- open faced omelette 54

F
Fillings for croissants, pita pockets, sandwiches, rolls, wraps 19
Fish
- parmesan crusted fish 48
- fresh tuna cakes 49
- tuna salad 68
- white fish filo parcels 50

French toast 10
Fresh green and red salad 64
Fresh tuna cakes 49
Fried rice 52
Frittata 53
Fruit muffins 80

G
Green pea and lettuce soup 30

H
Hash browns 11

I
Icecream
- banana soft freeze icecream 90
- coffee icecream 91
- maple icecream 92

J
Jam, rhubarb 98

L
Lamb balls 37
Lamb shanks 36
Larb - Thai meat salad 65
Leek & potato soup (vichyssoise) 32
Lentils, tasty 72
Little cheese muffins 87

M
Maple icecream 92
Mashed sweet potato 70
Mayonnaise 102
Meat
- beef casserole 34, 35
- lamb shanks 36
- Larb - Thai meat salad 65
- meat (beef, lamb or pork) or chicken balls 37
- savoury mince 38
- shepherd's pie 40

Mini quiche in bread cases 20
Mini upside down pear cakes 93
Muesli bars 81
Muffins & scones
- fruit muffins 80
- little cheese muffins 87
- savoury drop scones 88

N
Nachos with mince, sour cream & cheese 21

O
Open faced omelette 54
Orzo chicken stir fry 45

P
Pancakes 12
Parsley pesto 22
Parmesan crusted fish 48
Pasta
- orzo chicken stir fry 45
- penne pasta with fresh greens 55

Pears
- mini upside down pear cakes 93
- pear cake 82
- pear & caramel cake 94, 95
- pear & rhubarb crumble 96
- savoury pear sauce 102

Pear & caramel cake 94
Pear & rhubarb crumble 96
Pear cake 82
Pear cakes, mini upside down 93
Pea risotto 56
Penne pasta with fresh greens 55
Pita crisps 24
Pizza with homemade base 25, 26
Poppy seed cupcakes 83
Poppy seed loaf 84
Potatoes
   hash browns 11
   potato salad 66
   potato souffle 71
Potato salad 66
Potato souffle 71

Q
Quiche with homemade base 27

R
Relish, rhubarb 99
Rhubarb
   rhubarb & apple cake 85, 86
   rhubarb jam 98
   rhubarb relish 99
Rhubarb & apple cake 85, 86
Rhubarb jam 98
Rhubarb relish 99
Rice
   fried rice 52
   pea risotto 56
   rice paper spring rolls 58, 59
   risotto cakes 57
   saffron rice 60
Rice paper spring rolls 58, 59
Risotto cakes 57
Roast garlic hummus 23

S
Saffron rice 60
Salad Lyonnaise 67

Salads
   Caesar salad 62
   cole slaw 63
   fresh green & red salad 64
   Larb - Thai meat salad 65
   potato salad 66
   salad Lyonnaise 67
   tuna salad 68
   warm pumpkin, green bean
   & feta salad 69
Savoury drop scones 88
Savoury mince 38
Savoury mince filling for pita pockets,
   flat bread & bread cases 39
Savoury pear sauce 102
Shepherd's pie 40
Soups
   chicken soup 30
   green pea & lettuce soup 31
   leek & potato soup (vichyssoise) .. 32

T
Tamarillo chutney 100
Tasty lentils 72
Thai meat salad - Larb 65
Toasted tartine 28
Tuna salad 68
Turkey tenderloins or
   breasts stuffed 46, 47

V
Vegetables
   mashed sweet potato 70
   potato souffle 71
   tasty lentils 72
   vegetables - green & root 73
Vinegar & oil salad dressing 103
Vinegar, soy sauce & oil dressing 103

W
Waffles 13
Warm pumpkin, green bean
   & feta salad 69
White fish filo parcels 50